T0193436

Order this book online at www.trafford.com
or email orders@trafford.com

Most Trafford titles are also available at major online book retailers.

Trafford
PUBLISHING® www.trafford.com

North America & international
toll-free: 1 888 232 4444 (USA & Canada)
fax: 812 355 4082

Our mission is to efficiently provide the world's finest, most comprehensive book publishing service, enabling every author to experience success. To find out how to publish your book, your way, and have it available worldwide, visit us online at www.trafford.com

ISBN: 978-1-4907-9783-0 (sc)
ISBN: 978-1-4907-9782-3 (e)

Print information available on the last page.

Trafford rev. 08/11/2020

FIX IT TIPSIE!

Felipe Cofreros Ph.D.

Fix It Tipsie!

Tipsie was a young dog. He liked to be with his friends Jackie and Brownie. They helped each other even in doing assignments.

One time, Tipsie's teacher asked him to report in his Science class.

"Tipsie, will you report to the class the Life Cycle of a Butterfly?" Tipsie's teacher asked him.

"Yes, Teacher." He answered politely.

Jackie and Brownie helped him prepare his report. It was late by the time they finished it.

"Thanks, we're finished. Come on, Jackie, we need to run home." Brownie said to Jackie. "Bye, Tipsie. See you tomorrow."

Jackie and Brownie ran home.

Tipsie went to bed after Jackie and Brownie left. He was so tired. He was soon asleep.

The following morning, Tipsie overslept. He looked for his report on the table where he left it. He could not find his report. He started to panic when he could not find it.

"Where's my report?" he exclaimed. "I just left it on the table last night."

He looked under the table. He looked into the trashcan near the table. It was not there.

"Where could my report be?" Tipsie cried.

He looked under the bed. He even emptied his bag thinking he might have kept it there. But, he could not find his report.

He called up Jackie and Brownie but they were gone. He did not know what to do.

"My teacher will surely get mad if I can't present my report." Tipsie mumbled.

"Mom, help! My Science report is missing." he called his mother for help. His mother came into his room and helped him look for the report.

She found the report on the table under the pile of crumbled papers. "Is this what you are looking for?" Tipsie's mother asked.

Tipsie looked at it and exclaimed,
"Yes, Mom, this is it!"

Without eating breakfast,
Tipsie ran fast to school. He
was almost late. He was fainting
when he reached his classroom.

He promised himself, he would
fix his things for school ready for
the next day before sleeping.

Tipsie told Jackie and Brownie
about the incident.

From then on, Jackie and Brownie
called him *Fix It Tipsie!*

Exercise 1: Check (✔) the sentence that describes the picture.

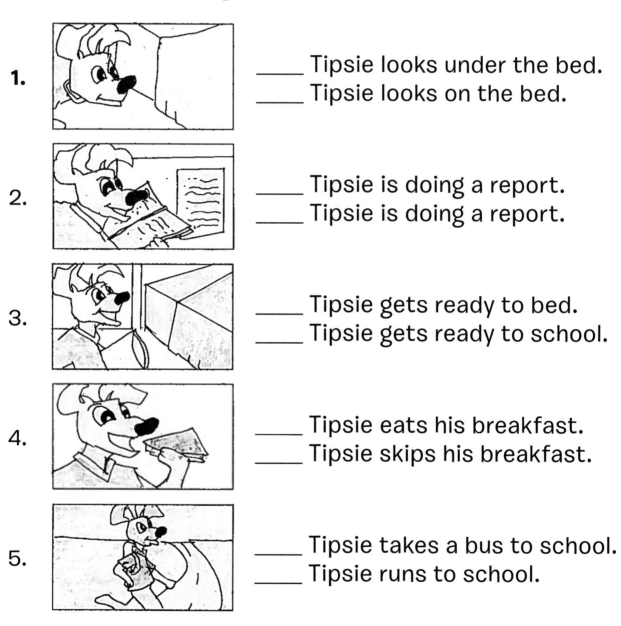

1. _____ Tipsie looks under the bed.
   _____ Tipsie looks on the bed.

2. _____ Tipsie is doing a report.
   _____ Tipsie is doing a report.

3. _____ Tipsie gets ready to bed.
   _____ Tipsie gets ready to school.

4. _____ Tipsie eats his breakfast.
   _____ Tipsie skips his breakfast.

5. _____ Tipsie takes a bus to school.
   _____ Tipsie runs to school.

Exercise 2: number the events.

_____ Jackie and Brownie helped Tipsie with his report.
_____ Tipsie went to bed and was soon asleep.
_____ Tipsie was assigned to do a report.
_____ Tipsie ran to school.
_____ Tipsie looked for his report in his bedroom.

Exercise 3: Check (✔) the things Tipsie should do and cross out (✗) the ones he should not do so that he would not be late to school.

FIX IT TIPSIE!

Felipe Cofreros Ph.D.

"FIX IT TIPSIE" is an eye-catching book that contains a story and more. This book is geared for pre-school children ages three and up. With the simple story and powerful comprehension questions, "FIX IT TIPSIE" engages the child by focusing concentration, improving comprehension, stimulating thought and galvanizing imagination.

This book is intended for use in the pre-school classroom. The students can answer questions, generate their own questions, act out the story or continue the story. It can be read to two and three year old students, while the older students can relate to the higher level activities.

Although the book is designed for classroom use, it can be used in the home, and setup in the book gives children a chance to relate to their parents while discussing the story.

Printed in the United States
By Bookmasters